ROOTED

[Discipleship Manual]

This Manual Belongs To:

_____

OTHER BOOKS BY JAKE KAIL

Restoring the Ministry of Jesus

How to Minister Deliverance [Training Manual]

Setting Captives Free

Hypocrisy Exposed

Keys for Deliverance

Discovering Your Destiny

Can a Christian Have a Demon?

Abiding in the Vine

Kids Empowered Curriculum

ROOTED

[Discipleship Manual]

Foundations for

Growing in Christ

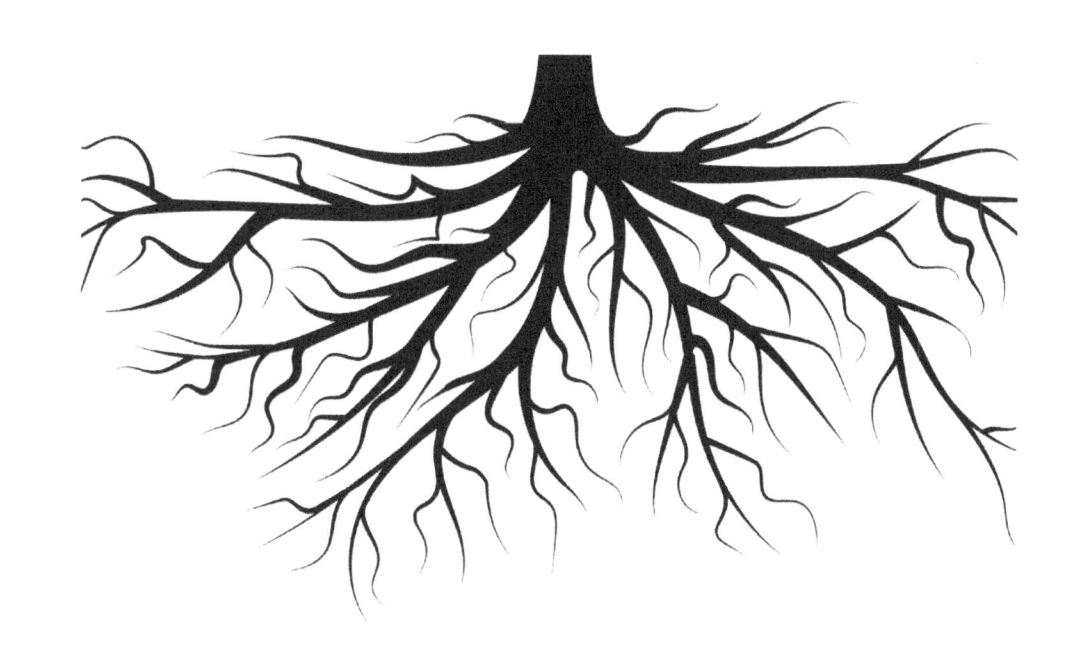

JAKE KAIL

Scripture taken from the New King James Version. Copyright © 1982 by Thomas Nelson, Inc. Used by permission.

Copyright © 2023 Jake Kail

All rights reserved. No part of this publication may be reproduced, stored in a retrieval system, or transmitted in any form or by any means, electronic, mechanical, photocopying, recording, or otherwise, without the prior written permission of the publisher.

www.jakekail.com

Acknowledgments

Thank you as always to my family—my wonderful wife, Anna, and our three amazing kids. I appreciate your encouragement and support in all of my writing projects!

Thank you to the Jake Kail Ministries intercessory prayer team. Your prayers are much appreciated! Thanks for praying for this manual throughout the writing and publishing process.

Thank you to my assistant, Kate Newcomer, for reviewing and editing the rough draft. Your attention to detail and input always enhances my writing projects!

Thank you to Erik Berling for helping with the cover design. I love how it turned out!

And most of all, thank you to our heavenly Father who leads us into deeper places of intimacy with Him and spiritual growth in Christ!

Contents

Introduction...9

Lesson 1: Being Rooted in Love..11

Lesson 2: The Purpose of Spiritual Disciplines..19

Lesson 3: Grounded in the Word..27

Lesson 4: Developing a Prayer Life..35

Lesson 5: The Spiritual Benefits of Fasting..43

Lesson 6: Knowing God in a Personal Way...51

Lesson 7: Empowered by the Holy Spirit...61

Lesson 8: Cultivating the Fruit of the Spirit...69

Lesson 9: Planted in the House of God..77

Lesson 10: Spiritual Growth through Kingdom Relationships............................85

Conclusion..93

Bonus Resources..95

About the Author..97

Introduction

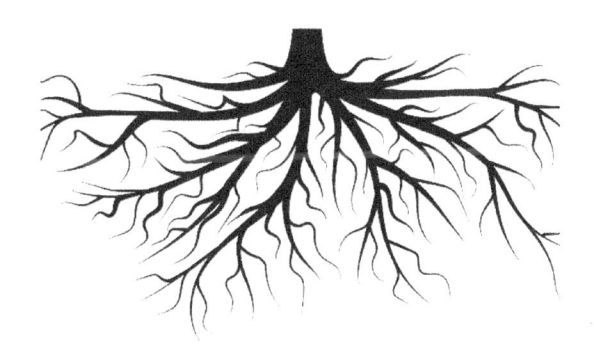

The focus of this discipleship manual is *spiritual growth*. Being saved and set free should be seen as a beginning, not an end. We are born again into God's Kingdom, and now we are called to know Him intimately, mature in Christ, and produce the fruit that He desires.

We are repeatedly admonished in Scripture to grow in our relationship with God:

- "But grow in the grace and knowledge of our Lord and Savior Jesus Christ." (2 Peter 3:18)

- "…that we should no longer be children, tossed to and fro and carried about with every wind of doctrine…but, speaking the truth in love, may grow up in all things into Him." (Ephesians 4:14-15)

- "Therefore, leaving the discussion of the elementary principles of Christ, let us go on to perfection…" (Hebrews 6:1)

In order to grow properly, we must be *rooted*. Consider a fruit tree. Roots are a part of the tree that are beneath the surface. They cannot be seen above the ground, but they are critical for the life, health, and growth of the tree. The root system provides stability and nourishment to the tree, enabling it to be healthy and produce fruit over time. In the same way, we must develop a *spiritual root system* that establishes us in Christ and empowers us to grow up in Him.

Spiritual growth does not happen by accident and neither does it happen overnight. It occurs as we are intentional in our daily practices of pursuing the Lord and following His ways. This discipleship manual is designed to equip you with the tools you need to mature in your walk with God. As you consistently put into practice the truths contained in this manual, you will grow steadily in your relationship with the Lord.

How to Use this Manual

This discipleship manual can be used for personal study and growth, small group teaching and discussion, or as a tool for discipling others. Each lesson is designed to teach and instruct but also to stir you to dig deeper into the Word for yourself, draw near to God, and take the next steps in your spiritual growth. The lessons contain segments of teaching interspersed with segments for reflection and application. These "Pause and Reflect" and "Dig Deeper" sections are important for digesting and assimilating the content and for personally applying what you are learning. So, don't breeze past these parts. Take time to ponder, journal, and seek the Lord. For group studies, this can be a time to pause the teaching and allow participants to get alone to reflect and apply the content before coming back together for more instruction and discussion.

Here are a few important points to keep in mind as you begin going through this manual:

- The topics within each lesson are covered in a foundational way and are not meant to be comprehensive in nature. Take advantage of the extra resources at the end of each lesson for further growth.

- Move through the manual at your own pace. Don't feel the need to rush through the lessons, but take time to let the subject matter sink in so that you can apply it to your life.

- If you are new to practicing spiritual disciplines, it might be daunting to try to add multiple disciplines at once. Give yourself grace for the journey. It might be helpful to add one discipline at a time to your life, and then add others once the first is established.

Whether for individuals or groups, this discipleship manual is designed to connect you with God and lead you further in your growth as a believer. May you encounter the Lord afresh as your roots go deeper into Him!

...

*Note that all Scripture references are taken from the New King James Version of the Bible.

Lesson 1

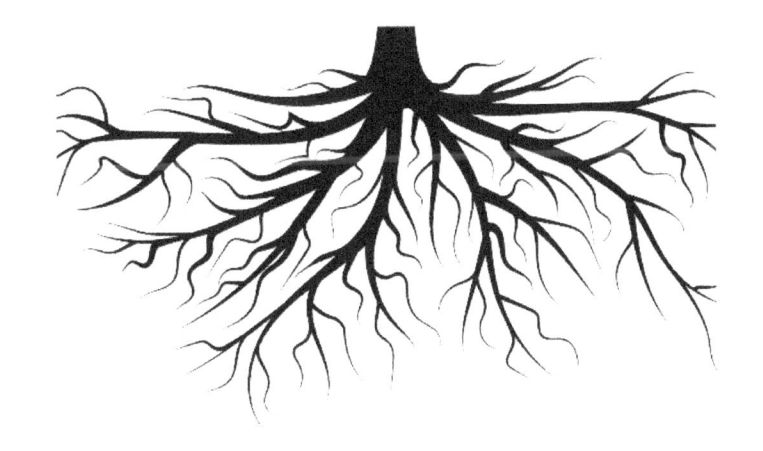

Being Rooted in Love

Opening Scripture

That He would grant you, according to the riches of His glory, to be strengthened with might through His Spirit in the inner man, that Christ may dwell in your hearts through faith; that you, being rooted and grounded in love, may be able to comprehend with all the saints what is the width and length and depth and height— to know the love of Christ which passes knowledge; that you may be filled with all the fullness of God. (Ephesians 3:16-19)

The opening Scripture of this lesson is a prayer of the apostle Paul for the Ephesian church. Notice that he specifically prayed that the Ephesian believers would be *rooted* and *grounded* in love. Let's look at these two words:

- Rooted: This speaks of the root system of a tree, which brings stability and nourishment.

- Grounded: This speaks of the foundation of a building, which brings security and strength.

The love of God is meant to keep us stable and secure—and it brings nourishment and strength to us. The choice of wording that Paul used shows us that God's love is *foundational*. Therefore, it is essential that we are rooted and grounded in the love of God as we seek to grow in Christ.

With God's love as our foundation, we can move forward in our walk with the Lord and mature as sons and daughters of God. But if we are not rooted in love, our pursuit of spiritual growth can easily become a religious duty or a legalistic burden without life or vitality.

When we are rooted and grounded in love:

- We work *from* the Father's love instead of *for* the Father's love.

- We see our circumstances through the lens of God's love, not God's love through the lens of our circumstances.

- We can remain stable in the midst of difficult and trying circumstances.

- We are secure as a child of God.

Pause and Reflect

Sometimes it is easy to believe that God loves people in a general sense but difficult to receive His love in a personal sense. In other words, we can affirm God's love for humanity while struggling to truly know and believe His love for us as an individual.

What is your current understanding and experience of God's love for you personally? Is it something you struggle to believe and receive, or does it come easily? Do you feel secure in His love?

_____
_____
_____

Lesson 1: Being Rooted in Love

The Foundation of Love

As we have already seen, love is a foundational issue in our walk with God. Consider also the following:

- Jesus said that the greatest commandments are to love God and love others (see Matthew 22:36-40).

- Without love, all of the gifts and power of the Holy Spirit are not profitable (see 1 Corinthians 13).

- Our love for God and others is a response to God's love for us (see 1 John 4:19).

We love God, because He first loved us. This means that our spiritual growth and intimacy with God are directly impacted by our present revelation of God's love for us personally. The deeper our revelation of the love of Christ, the more we can be filled with the fullness of God, for God is love (see 1 John 4:8).

> **"...to know the love of Christ which passes knowledge; that you may be filled with all the fullness of God." (Ephesians 3:19)**

Paul says that we are to know Christ's love but then says that it surpasses knowledge! What does this mean? The word for *know* in the original Greek speaks of experiential knowledge. I believe Paul is saying that the full scope of God's love is beyond human comprehension (knowledge) but that we can know it by experience in deeper and deeper depths.

As we know God's love in greater measure, we are "rooted and grounded in love" in an increasing way. His love sustains us and creates stability. It becomes the foundation upon which our lives are built.

Pause and Reflect

Sometimes there are past experiences, mindsets, or other factors hindering us from truly knowing and experiencing God's love for us.

Can you think of anything hindering you from experiencing or walking in God's love for you? How has your relationship with parents or other authority figures impacted your view of God in a positive or negative way? Are there circumstances you have walked through that have caused you to question His love?

_____
_____
_____
_____
_____
_____
_____
_____
_____
_____
_____
_____
_____
_____

Lesson 1: Being Rooted in Love

_____
_____
_____
_____
_____
_____
_____
_____
_____
_____
_____
_____
_____
_____
_____
_____
_____
_____
_____
_____

How Do We Become Rooted in God's Love?

Like all spiritual growth, being rooted and grounded in God's love can be a process. If it were automatic, Paul would not have prayed for the Ephesians to experience this in increasing amounts. So, ask God to reveal His love to you by the Holy Spirit and through His Word.

Below are two ways that will help us to grow in being rooted in God's love:

1. When we believe what the Bible says about the love of God

The Scriptures have many promises and statements about God's great love for His people. But if we do not believe what the Bible says, we will not truly know His love for us. When we believe God's Word, it helps to root us in His love. We begin to see that our circumstances do not determine His love for us.

The greatest demonstration of God's love for us is found in the cross of Christ.

> **"But God demonstrates His own love toward us, in that while we were still sinners, Christ died for us." (Romans 5:8)**

God did not just *say* that He loves us—He *demonstrated* it!

2. When we experience God's love in personal ways

"Oh, taste and see that the Lord is good; Blessed is the man who trusts in Him!" (Psalm 34:8)

The words *taste* and *see* speak of experience. We are not simply to know intellectually that God is good and that He loves us; we are to taste this for ourselves. There are certainly times when we simply must trust in His goodness regardless of what we see, feel, or experience. But we are also to experience His love in a tangible way.

The Bible says that the love of God is poured into our hearts by the Holy Spirit (see Romans 5:5). God loves us whether we feel it or not—but there are times when we encounter His love in a more perceptible way, and when this happens, our roots go deeper into Him.

We can experience God's love when:

- We feel His presence in a time of worship or prayer

- He answers a prayer or confirms something in a specific and personal way

- Other people love us in a sacrificial way and His love comes through

- We receive a miracle, experience deliverance or healing, or see His provision

As we become more rooted in God's love, our lives are placed on a solid foundation. This prepares the way for us to grow in a deeper relationship with the Lord and mature in Him.

Dig Deeper

Read and meditate on Luke 15:11-32. Ask the Holy Spirit to teach you and give you a deeper revelation of the Father's love. Write down anything that God shows you through these verses.

_____
_____
_____
_____
_____
_____
_____

Ask the Holy Spirit to show you if you have roots in things other than God's love. Write down anything He reveals to you, and then ask Him to help you to remove these roots and place them in God's love and truth.

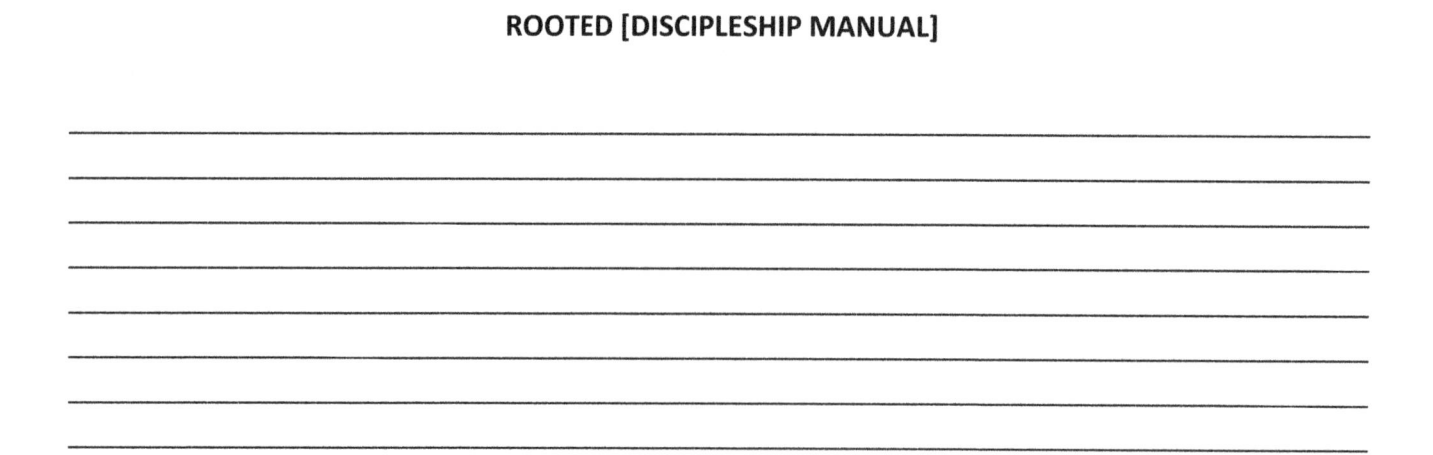

For Further Growth

Audio Sermon: Rooted in God's Love

Lesson 2

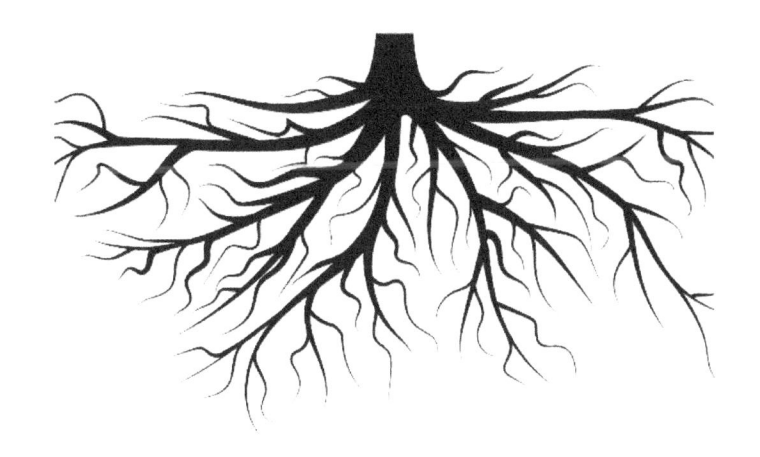

The Purpose of Spiritual Disciplines

Opening Scripture

But reject profane and old wives' fables, and exercise yourself toward godliness. For bodily exercise profits a little, but godliness is profitable for all things, having promise of the life that now is and of that which is to come. (1 Timothy 4:7-8)

The opening Scripture for this lesson compares growing in godliness to physical exercise. One of the similarities between spiritual growth and exercise is that they both require *discipline.*

Spiritual disciplines are certain practices that we can do as believers in order to grow in our relationship with God. A spiritual discipline is a way to prioritize our growth as believers in Christ. These should not be seen as an end in themselves but as a means to spiritual growth and intimacy with God. We will cover various spiritual disciplines in more depth throughout this manual, but some examples include prayer, studying the Bible, and fasting.

Why do we need discipline in order to grow in our relationship with God? The fact is, spiritual growth does not happen by accident and neither does it happen overnight. It transpires over time through consistency and intentional effort on our part. There are various forces that oppose our walk with God and growth in Christ. The world is full of distractions that can easily pull us off course if we are not careful. The devil seeks to assail us with temptations and lies. And our own flesh resists our spiritual progress, trying to lull us into selfishness or sin. Discipline is a must for our spiritual growth!

- Discipline, in a general sense, means short-term pain or discomfort for long-term benefit (see Hebrews 12:11).

- Discipline implies intentional effort, sacrifice, consistency, and focus (see 1 Corinthians 9:24-27).

- Discipline means we do something even when we don't feel like it or understand it fully.

Pause and Reflect

Growing in our relationship with God is the most worthwhile pursuit we can engage in, but it doesn't always come easy. There are things that can hinder us from being disciplined in our walk with God.

How has your experience with spiritual disciplines been? What obstacles have you faced in developing spiritual disciplines in your life? How can you be intentional to overcome these obstacles?

_____
_____
_____
_____
_____
_____
_____
_____

Lesson 2: The Purpose of Spiritual Disciplines

_____
_____
_____
_____
_____
_____
_____
_____
_____
_____
_____
_____
_____
_____
_____
_____
_____
_____
_____
_____
_____
_____
_____
_____
_____

Two Purposes of Spiritual Disciplines

Exercising spiritual disciplines should not be seen as the end goal in itself. Disciplines are a means to an end. There are two primary purposes for spiritual disciplines that we will cover in this lesson.

1. Growing up in Christ

Getting saved is the beginning of our spiritual life. The Bible describes this as being "born again" (see John 3:1-8). Salvation is the *beginning* of our Christian journey. We are not meant to stay spiritual babies but to grow up in Christ.

Just as a natural child needs certain ingredients to grow and be healthy, the same is true spiritually. If a perfectly healthy newborn is neglected or not fed properly, they will not survive or grow up healthily. Spiritual disciplines provide the necessary ingredients for continued spiritual growth.

It is important to understand that maturing in Christ does not happen by the mere passing of time. It happens through a process of intentional and consistent spiritual practices over the course of our lives. As we mature, we begin to take on certain characteristics such as godly character, stability in our relationship with God, and increasing wisdom.

2. Intimacy with God

I believe that the highest purpose of spiritual disciplines is to know God more intimately. The apostle Paul explained that he was always pressing forward into a deeper knowledge of Christ (see Philippians 3:7-8). Spiritual disciplines provide a context for relationship to occur. In other words, the purpose of discipline is to make room for relationship.

For example, when we are intentional to regularly spend time alone with God in prayer and reading the Bible, it creates space for our relationship with God to grow. It takes discipline to maintain this practice, but discipline is not the ultimate goal, growing in our relationship with the Lord is.

Focusing on the relationship will keep us from slipping into legalism or ritualism.

- Legalism: trying to approach God or base our salvation on the basis of our own good works or effort
    - We must always approach God through the blood of Jesus. Spiritual disciplines are not a way to earn His love but to grow in relationship with Him.

- Ritualism: going through the motions of spiritual practices without our heart being engaged
    - Spiritual disciplines are not religious routines to check off the list but a way to engage with God and know Him more.

Pause and Reflect

Sometimes we get in a rut in our spiritual disciplines and need to recalibrate our hearts and our routines.

Have you ever found yourself falling into legalism or ritualism in your relationship with God? How can you embrace spiritual disciplines while avoiding these two pitfalls?

_____
_____
_____
_____
_____
_____

Lesson 2: The Purpose of Spiritual Disciplines

Spiritual Discipline vs. Spiritual Hunger

> "...as newborn babes, desire the pure milk of the word, that you may grow thereby." (1 Peter 2:2)

Something else to consider is the value of *spiritual hunger*. Peter encourages our desire for the Word to be like a newborn's desire to be fed with milk. When we have an intense spiritual hunger, the need for discipline is less because our hunger drives us to draw near to God, pray, read His Word, and other spiritual practices.

I have had seasons of strong spiritual hunger and seasons where hunger has waned. In the seasons where hunger is less, I still have the discipline to fall back on. This is one of the reasons why establishing spiritual disciplines is key to our continual growth. It keeps us growing and moving forward even in times when we don't feel like it. So, establish spiritual disciplines and also cultivate spiritual hunger.

- Establish spiritual disciplines:
    - Make a decision to prioritize your spiritual growth and relationship with God above everything else in your life.
    - Decide what spiritual disciplines you need to grow in and make a practical plan for how you will implement these disciplines.
    - Follow through by consistently engaging in spiritual disciplines, even in times when you don't feel like it.
    - Give yourself grace for the journey and don't expect perfection.

- Cultivate spiritual hunger:
    - Ask God to give you a greater hunger for Him, His Word, and for spiritual growth.
    - Don't allow yourself to be satisfied with the lesser things of this world—be determined to be satisfied by God alone.
    - Ask God to draw you closer to Him and to reveal Himself to you in a greater way.

Dig Deeper

Read and meditate on Hebrews 12:1-13. Ask the Holy Spirit to teach you and give you a deeper revelation of endurance and spiritual discipline. Write down anything that God shows you through these verses.

_____
_____
_____
_____
_____
_____
_____
_____
_____

Lesson 2: The Purpose of Spiritual Disciplines

Take time to reflect on your current relationship with God and how you have incorporated spiritual disciplines into your life. Ask the Holy Spirit to show you if there are any spiritual disciplines He wants you to add or increase in your life and write down anything He shows you. Ask the Lord to increase your spiritual hunger and to show you anything that is hindering you from hungering for Him.

For Further Growth

Audio Sermon: Running with Endurance

Lesson 3

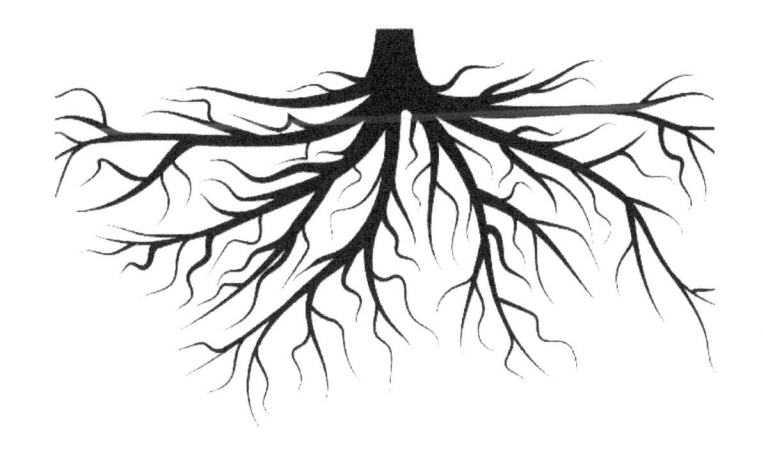

Grounded in the Word

Opening Scripture

Therefore, laying aside all malice, all deceit, hypocrisy, envy, and all evil speaking, as newborn babes, desire the pure milk of the word, that you may grow thereby, if indeed you have tasted that the Lord is gracious. (1 Peter 2:1-3)

As stated in the previous lesson and seen in this lesson's opening Scripture, Peter encourages believers to hunger for the Word just as an infant hungers for their mother's milk. Notice that he also directly connects this to our spiritual growth: "that you may grow thereby."

As Christians, we are often exhorted to read the Bible. But without understanding the reasons *why* reading the Word is so important, we can lack motivation and/or only do it out of a religious duty. When we understand why reading the Bible is so important, we can begin to engage in this spiritual discipline with more intentionality and focus.

- The Bible gives us commands and guidelines, but it is more than a list of rules to follow.

- The Bible teaches us what is true and what is not, but it is more than a set of doctrines to believe.

- The Bible shows us many promises of God to His people, but it is more than a group of promises to claim.

God's Word is living, active, and powerful (see Hebrews 4:12). The Scriptures are foundational to our relationship with God and are meant to draw us into deeper fellowship with Him. It is essential that we take regular time to read, study, and meditate on the Scriptures. We will cover various reasons why this is so important later in this lesson, but first let's reflect on the significance of Scripture in our lives.

Pause and Reflect

While not an exact parallel, our attitude toward the Bible is often indicative of the condition of our relationship with God.

How would you describe your attitude toward Scripture? Have you ever experienced hunger for God's Word? What has been your pattern of reading and studying the Bible?

_____
_____
_____
_____
_____
_____
_____
_____
_____
_____

Lesson 3: Grounded in the Word

_____
_____
_____
_____
_____
_____
_____
_____
_____
_____
_____
_____
_____
_____
_____
_____
_____
_____
_____
_____
_____
_____
_____
_____

Reasons to Spend Regular Time in the Word

When we understand why reading the Bible is so important, it will help to motivate us to engage in this important spiritual discipline. While not an exhaustive list, below are several reasons why studying the Bible is foundational to our walk with God and growth as believers.

1. Revelation of God (see 2 Timothy 3:16-17)

- The Bible is inspired by God and a primary way that He speaks to us. It is God's revelation of Himself to mankind. Therefore, spending regular time in the Scriptures is key for growing in our relationship with Him. If we want to get to know God, His nature, His will, and His ways, we must consistently invest time in the Word.

2. Spiritual nourishment (see 1 Peter 2:2; Matthew 4:4)

- The Word of God is compared to milk, bread, and solid food. The symbolism is clear: as good food nourishes our body, the Word of God nourishes our spirit. Here is an important tip to remember: *even if you don't remember or understand everything you read, it still nourishes your spirit!*

3. A solid foundation (see Psalm 1:1-3; Matthew 7:24-25)

- The Word is a solid foundation to build our lives upon. Being grounded in the Word keeps us firmly rooted, protects us from deception, and enables us to be strong during trials. Without this foundation, we are susceptible to being drawn into error or being derailed by the storms of life.

4. A weapon against the enemy/temptation (see Ephesians 6:17; Matthew 4:1-11; Psalm 119:11)

- When Jesus was tempted by the devil, He overcame each temptation the same way: by quoting Scripture. God's Word is a sword to help stand against the enemy and be victorious over temptation. But if we don't know the Word, we cannot use it as a sword in spiritual battle.

5. Cleansing and sanctification (see Psalm 119:9; John 17:17; Ephesians 5:26)

- God's Word has a cleansing effect on us. Spending time reading and studying the Bible can be likened to taking a spiritual bath. God uses His Word to continue the process of sanctification in us—this means that His Word helps us to become more holy.

Pause and Reflect

Of the five reasons to regularly study the Bible, which one stands out to you the most and why? How have you seen the power of God's Word at work in one of these five ways? Are there any other reasons you can think of to regularly study the Scriptures?

_____
_____
_____
_____
_____
_____
_____

How Should I Study the Bible?

The Bible is a big book! Many believers might find it intimidating to know how best to study and read the Bible or question whether they are able to comprehend and apply it properly. Know that reading, understanding, and applying the Scriptures is a lifelong process. We will be growing in this discipline for the remainder of our lives. Take it one step and one day at a time. Also know that God will help give understanding of His Word as you set your heart to seek Him and know Him more. Always ask for the guidance and revelation of the Holy Spirit when you read the Bible (see Luke 24:45).

One practical thing you can do as you study the Bible is to seek to determine three aspects:

1. Revelation: what the passage says

2. Interpretation: what the passage means

3. Application: how the passage applies to your life

Take your time to meditate on passages of Scripture you are reading. Don't be in a hurry to simply check Bible reading off of your list for the day. If you come across a passage that seems confusing or one that you don't understand, ask God for insight. But also know that it is okay to not have it all figured out, so don't get bogged down. You can move forward and trust that the Holy Spirit will bring more insight in due time.

In addition to the above, consider three ways that you can study the Bible:

1. Front to back: going through a whole book of the Bible, the Old Testament or New Testament, or the entire Bible

- This is an important way to study God's Word, because it ensures that we are reading the whole Bible and not simply gravitating to personal favorite passages. I personally make this my default way of studying the Scriptures.

2. Topical study: picking a topic to study and finding various passages that relate to it

- This can be helpful when the Lord is highlighting a specific theme or topic that He is wanting us to grow in. There are major themes of the Bible that have insights scattered throughout various parts. You can dig into a subject and get deeper insight by looking at numerous places that deal with the topic.

3. Spontaneous passage: being drawn by the Holy Spirit to a specific passage

- Sometimes the Holy Spirit will lead you to a specific Bible verse or portion of Scripture spontaneously. This can often happen when the Lord is wanting to speak into a specific situation in your life and teach you something. Be sensitive to lean into these moments and dig into what the Lord might be communicating to you.

Dig Deeper

Read and meditate on Psalm 119. Ask the Holy Spirit to teach you and give you a greater hunger and love for God's Word. Write down anything that God shows you through these verses.

Lesson 3: Grounded in the Word

How satisfied are you with your current pattern of reading the Bible? Ask the Holy Spirit to lead you into how to study the Bible in this season and what it looks like to prioritize this spiritual discipline. Write down any thoughts on how to intentionally plan for how and when to read the Bible on a regular basis.

For Further Growth

Video Sermon: Feeding on God's Word

Lesson 4

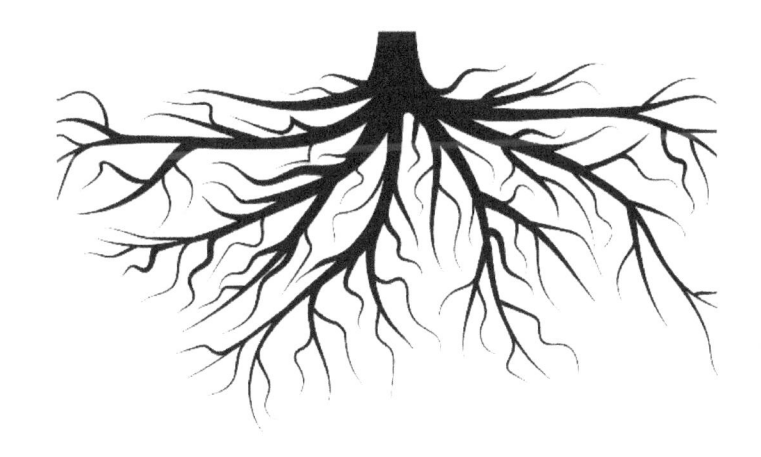

Developing a Prayer Life

Opening Scripture

But you, when you pray, go into your room, and when you have shut your door, pray to your Father who is in the secret place; and your Father who sees in secret will reward you openly. (Matthew 6:6)

In this lesson's opening Scripture, Jesus is teaching about the importance of prayer. He explains that we are to shut out distractions and go to the "secret place" to meet with our Father in heaven. Jesus not only taught the value of prayer—He lived it. He would often get away from the crowds to pray (see Mark 1:35; Luke 5:16).

Prayer is one of the most important activities we can do as Christians. Yet, developing a prayer life seems to be one of the hardest things for many believers to do. If we are going to grow in our relationship with God, prayer must become a top priority for us.

- Prayer is at the same time a simple and multi-faceted subject.
    - It is simple in that it is a conversation with God.
    - It is multi-faceted in that there are various types of prayer, conditions for answered prayer, and nuances to prayer.

- Prayer is communication with God, communion with God, and union with God.
    - Ultimately, prayer is about relationship with God. It is about getting to know Him more.

- There are various types of prayer.
    - We can praise and worship God, offer thanksgiving, confess sin, ask for petitions and requests, intercede on behalf of others, have conversation with God, listen and wait on the Lord, pray in tongues, and more.

Pause and Reflect

Developing a prayer life does not happen overnight. It takes time and intentionality to learn how to pray and to make prayer a regular practice.

Where are you at on the journey of being a person of prayer? What place has prayer had in your life and relationship with God?

_____
_____
_____
_____
_____
_____
_____
_____

Developing a Prayer Life

Growing a prayer life will certainly require discipline. But remember, discipline is not the goal, relationship is. Learning how to pray effectively and receive answers to prayer is also important, but I believe that knowing God intimately is the highest purpose of prayer.

We must aim to make personal devotion to God in the secret place the highest priority of our lives. In order to be growing and thriving, our personal devotion should be:

1. Intentional → We must set aside the time for prayer.

- A prayer life does not develop by accident. It will happen as we are intentional to make it a priority. Practically speaking, this means that we should schedule it into our day. Don't wait until you have some spare minutes. Pick a time that works well with your life and schedule, and set it as your personal time with God.

2. Focused → We must be free of distraction.

- Jesus said that when we pray, we should go into our room and shut the door (see Matthew 6:6). This speaks of setting aside distractions so that we can be focused. Put away your phone, set aside responsibilities, and keep other distractions out of mind as best as you can.

3. Consistent → We must make prayer a regular practice.

- In order to develop a prayer life, we must make prayer a consistent practice. I strongly recommend making time in the secret place a *daily* priority. Fight to stay consistent in the secret place!

Pause and Reflect

The above section named three keys for growing in prayer. Which of these three do you feel the strongest in? Which one is the most challenging? What can you do to make prayer a more consistent spiritual discipline in your life?

_____
_____
_____
_____
_____
_____
_____
_____
_____
_____
_____
_____
_____
_____
_____
_____
_____
_____
_____

Structuring Your Time with God

It is helpful to have a basic structure for your times in the secret place while also remaining flexible and sensitive to the Holy Spirit's leading. Below are some examples of potential structures:

Example 1:

- Praise and thanksgiving
- Time in the Word
- Intercessory prayer

Example 2:

- Time in the Word
- Journaling what God is speaking
- Praise, thanksgiving, and intercession

Example 3:

- Praying in tongues
- Prayer and intercession
- Time in the Word

Example 4:

- Waiting on God
- Time in the Word
- Praise, prayer, and intercession

I encourage you to develop a structure for your prayer times that works for you. The purpose of the structure is to give you a basic track to follow, but you don't need to be rigid about it. Always be open to how the Holy Spirit may lead during your prayer time. Also, be aware that the Lord may lead you into different structures in different seasons.

Dig Deeper

Read and meditate on Matthew 6:5-13. Ask the Holy Spirit to teach you and give you deeper insight into the blessing and power of prayer. Write down anything that God shows you through these verses.

Do you have a basic structure for your times of prayer? How has that structure changed during different periods in your life? Take time to reflect and ask the Holy Spirit if there is a structure for your times in the secret place that is right for this season.

For Further Growth

Video Sermon: A Call to the Secret Place

Audio Sermon: Partnering with God Through Prayer

Lesson 5

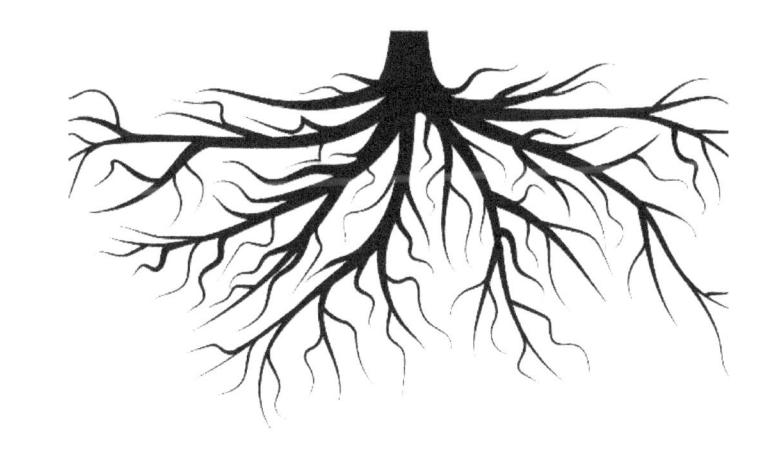

The Spiritual Benefits of Fasting

Opening Scripture

Moreover, when you fast, do not be like the hypocrites, with a sad countenance. For they disfigure their faces that they may appear to men to be fasting. Assuredly, I say to you, they have their reward. But you, when you fast, anoint your head and wash your face, so that you do not appear to men to be fasting, but to your Father who is in the secret place; and your Father who sees in secret will reward you openly. (Matthew 6:16-18)

ROOTED [DISCIPLESHIP MANUAL]

One of the primary spiritual disciplines is *fasting*. Simply put, fasting is to abstain from food for a spiritual purpose. It is clear from the opening Scripture that Jesus expected His followers to fast. He said, "When you fast" not "If you fast." It is also clear that our motives must be pure for us to obtain the benefits of fasting that God intends.

- Fasting was practiced by many of the heroes of the faith.
    - Moses, Daniel, and Esther are a few examples.

- Fasting was practiced and taught by Jesus.
    - See Matthew 4:1-2; Matthew 6:16-18

- Fasting was practiced by the early church.
    - See Acts 13:1-3

The basic premise of fasting is to abstain from food for a spiritual purpose. Sometimes people might also fast from things such as entertainment, social media, or other activities. It can be helpful to fast from other things like this in order to give more time and attention to the Lord. But from a biblical perspective, fasting is technically about forgoing physical nourishment.

We can see various ways that people fasted in the Bible, and three main types of fasting are listed below.

1. The Total Fast → abstaining from all food and all liquids for a period of time

- Biblical example: Esther (see Esther 4:16)
- The total fast is not a common fast, as in most cases of fasting liquids are consumed. This type of fast should only be entered into by a clear leading of the Holy Spirit and only for a short time.

2. The Normal Fast → abstaining from all food and liquids except water (or other liquids)

- Biblical example: Jesus (see Matthew 4:1-2)
- This is a main way to fast on a regular basis. You can abstain from all solid foods for a set period of time. You can also choose to abstain from all liquids except water if you feel led.

3. The Partial Fast → abstaining from specific food items (such as meats) for a period of time

- Biblical example: Daniel (see Daniel 10:3)
- This is sometimes called a *Daniel Fast* based on his example. This type of fast normally involves abstaining from all food except for fruits and vegetables (no meats or sweets!). This is a great

way to do an extended fast (such as 21 days) and is also a great way for those who cannot participate in a normal fast due to health reasons.

Pause and Reflect

While fasting is an important and basic spiritual discipline, it has often been neglected in the modern church. Some might see it as extreme or only for "super-spiritual" believers. But as we have seen, Jesus saw it as a normal practice for His disciples.

Have you incorporated fasting into your walk with God? If so, how has your experience with fasting been? Have you tried any different types of fasting or lengths of time?

_____
_____
_____
_____
_____
_____
_____
_____
_____
_____
_____
_____
_____
_____
_____
_____
_____
_____
_____
_____
_____
_____
_____
_____
_____

Four Spiritual Benefits of Fasting

Fasting is not usually a physically pleasant experience. Aside from hunger, it is also often accompanied by headaches, bad breath, and weariness of body and mind. So why would anyone want to voluntarily abstain from food? In this section, we will look at some of the spiritual benefits of fasting.

1. Drawing Near to God (see James 4:8)

- Fasting helps us to set aside time to be with the Lord. It is one of the ways that we can draw near to God with expectation that He will draw near to us. It helps us focus on the Lord and can be a way to recalibrate spiritually.

2. Overcoming the Flesh (see Galatians 5:16-17)

- Fasting prioritizes the spirit over the body. Since you are abstaining from food, which is a basic human need, you are exercising self-control. This helps translate for overcoming the flesh in general and putting to death selfish desires. If you can have self-control in fasting, you can overcome other areas.

3. Humbling Ourselves (see Psalm 35:13)

- We are called to humble *ourselves*, and fasting is one of the ways we can intentionally do this. Fasting puts us in a weakened condition. It demonstrates dependence on God and His Word and is one of the biblical ways to humble ourselves before the Lord.

4. Obtaining Spiritual Breakthrough (see Mark 9:29)

- Fasting has an impact on the spiritual realm. There are times when fasting can bring a breakthrough that prayer alone will not obtain. The simple act of fasting does spiritual war against the enemy and helps us to walk in victory.

Lesson 5: The Spiritual Benefits of Fasting

Pause and Reflect

The above section named four spiritual benefits of fasting. Which of these four sticks out to you the most and why? Can you think of any situations where a time of fasting brought a spiritual breakthrough in your life? Are there any specific prayer requests or situations that you want to commit to fasting for?

_____
_____
_____
_____
_____
_____
_____
_____
_____
_____
_____
_____
_____
_____
_____
_____
_____
_____
_____
_____
_____
_____
_____
_____
_____
_____

Lesson 5: The Spiritual Benefits of Fasting

Practical Tips for Fasting

Believers have various experiences with fasting. Some have powerful encounters with God during times of fasting. Others see the fruit after the fast is complete. Sometimes we may not know what the result of our fasting is. But we can be sure of this: any time we fast with pure motives, we are drawing near to God, obeying Him, and impacting our spiritual life and those around us.

Maybe you have never fasted before or perhaps you are a veteran. Here are some practical points to help you on your fasting journey.

1. If you have never fasted before, start small and work towards longer fasts.

- Think of fasting like exercise. If you have never gone running before, you wouldn't start with running a marathon on your first day! Be led by the Holy Spirit, but generally it is good to start small and build up to longer periods of fasting.

2. If you have health issues that would limit your ability to fast, don't disregard them.

- Certain health conditions can impact a person's ability to fast. Also, nursing or pregnant mothers are not able to fast in a normal way. If you fall into one of these categories, you can still fast in creative ways (e.g., partial fast or fasting one meal). Use wisdom and caution in these matters.

3. If you are coming off of a long fast, ease yourself back in to regular eating.

- When you fast for an extended period of time, your digestive system shuts down and your stomach shrinks. It can be tempting to break a long fast with a large meal, but your body will not respond well to this! Ease back in to eating slowly with foods that are easy to digest.

4. Make fasting a regular part of your Christian walk.

- Like any other spiritual discipline, consistency is key. Make fasting a regular practice. This can look different in different seasons, but here are some different possibilities.
    - Fast one day per week
    - Do a three-day fast each month
    - Fast a certain number of meals each week
    - Do a 21-day fast once a year

5. Give yourself grace!

- As you grow in the discipline of fasting, make sure to give yourself plenty of grace. Remember, spiritual disciplines are not meant to be legalistic burdens or ritualistic routines. Ask God to give you a greater grace to fast and step out into this important spiritual practice!

Dig Deeper

Read and meditate on Isaiah 58. Ask the Holy Spirit to teach you and give you revelation into the heart posture for fasting that pleases God. Write down anything that God shows you through these verses.

_____
_____
_____
_____
_____
_____
_____
_____
_____
_____
_____
_____
_____
_____
_____
_____
_____
_____
_____
_____
_____
_____
_____
_____

Ask the Holy Spirit to show you what fasting is supposed to look like for you and your walk with God. Ask Him to give you grace for fasting. Write down any thoughts on how you plan to incorporate fasting into your life on a regular basis.

_____
_____
_____
_____
_____
_____
_____
_____
_____
_____
_____
_____
_____
_____
_____
_____
_____
_____

For Further Growth

Video Sermon: The Purpose and Power of Fasting

Lesson 6

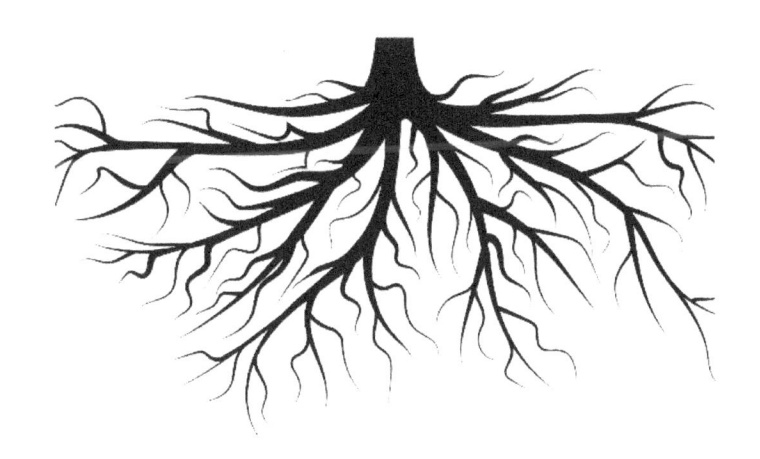

Knowing God in a Personal Way

Opening Scripture

And this is eternal life, that they may know You, the only true God, and Jesus Christ whom You have sent. (John 17:3)

In this lesson's opening Scripture, Jesus gives a definition of what it means to have eternal life. Notice that He does not say that eternal life means to live forever in heaven. While heaven is the eternal home of believers, Jesus defines eternal life in a different way: to know God personally.

The Christian walk is a relationship with God. We are meant to not simply know things *about* God but to actually know Him. Through our salvation in Christ, we are forgiven of our sins so that we can be reconciled to the Father and walk in fellowship with Him.

Fundamental to knowing God is understanding His nature. The Bible reveals various aspects of God's nature. Recognizing these facets of who God reveals Himself to be is an important aspect of knowing Him. Let's look at a few of these character traits.

- God is love (see 1 John 4:8).
    - The essence of God's nature is love; all He does is out of love.

- God is holy (see 1 Peter 1:16).
    - God is set apart from all others, and He is perfect in holiness.

- God is good (see Psalm 34:8).
    - God is full of goodness, and everything He does is good.

- God is sovereign (see Psalm 99:1-3).
    - God is the supreme ruler over all. He is eternal, and there is none higher than Him.

- God is just (see Psalm 89:14).
    - God is righteous and just in all His ways and all His judgments.

Pause and Reflect

While it is important to have accurate knowledge about God, there is a difference between knowing things about God and knowing God in a personal way. And while experience is not the foundation of doctrine, we are meant to know God in an experiential way.

Where are you at in your journey of knowing God in a personal way? What are some tangible ways that you have experienced God? Are there ways that you desire to know God in a more experiential way?

_____
_____
_____
_____

Experiencing God's Presence

One of the ways that we can get to know God more personally is by experiencing His presence. God's *omnipresence* means that He is everywhere. But His *manifest presence* is when He reveals His presence in a tangible way. As believers, we have access to the manifest presence of God, and we can grow in and live in this reality.

As Jesus died on the cross, something very significant happened:

> "And Jesus cried out with a loud voice, and breathed His last. Then the veil of the temple was torn in two from top to bottom." (Mark 15:37-38)

The veil in the Old Testament temple separated people from the manifest presence of God. Only the high priest could go through the veil and enter the Most Holy Place, and only one time per year. But through His body and blood, Jesus made the way for us to come into God's presence (see Hebrews 10:19-22). As believers, we should expect to experience God's manifest presence.

While we cannot make God reveal Himself, we can seek His face in an intentional way. The Bible says that as we draw near to Him, He will draw near to us (see James 4:8). Here are some keys for experiencing God's presence in deeper ways.

- Thirst (see John 7:37)
    - As we desire God and recognize our need for Him, we will seek Him, draw near to Him, and position ourselves to receive from Him.

- Priority (see Luke 10:38-42)
    - Mary prioritized the presence of Jesus while Martha was distracted and busy with serving. All believers have access to God's presence, but those who prioritize His presence will experience His presence.

- Faith (see Hebrews 11:6)
    - When we approach God, we must truly believe that He is there and that He is hearing our prayers and responding to our pursuit of knowing Him more. We come to Him in faith, based on His Word.

- Persistence (see Hebrews 11:6)
    - God rewards those who are *diligent* in seeking Him. It is not the casual or flippant who encounter God's presence but those who persistently and diligently seek Him.

Pause and Reflect

There are various ways that people may experience the tangible presence of God, and we shouldn't compare our journey with others or expect that it must look identical to another person's experience. Some examples could include having a tangible physical sensation, being filled with love, experiencing deep peace or joy, weeping in His presence, or encountering a powerful awe and reverence for God's holiness.

What does it mean for you to experience the presence of God? Are there specific ways that God manifests His presence to you? What does it look like for you to prioritize God's presence and diligently seek Him?

Hearing God's Voice

Throughout the Bible we see God as One who speaks. One of the ways that we grow in intimacy with the Lord is through hearing His voice. Christianity is about relationship with God, and this includes hearing God speak and being led by the Holy Spirit.

"My sheep hear My voice, and I know them, and they follow Me." (John 10:27)

Learning to recognize God's voice is a process. But as we draw near to Him and He draws near to us, we can grow in hearing and following His voice. Below is a list of some of the common ways that God communicates with His people.

1. The Bible (see 2 Timothy 3:16)

- The primary and most foundational way that God speaks to us is through the Bible. Anything that God says to us will be in line with the overall counsel of His Word and will never contradict it. If we want to grow in recognizing God's voice, we must be students of the Word.

2. The Still Small Voice (see 1 Kings 19:12)

- This is when God speaks in the form of an impression, inspired thought, gentle whisper, or quiet nudge of the Holy Spirit. It can be subtle, so we must be alert to tune in to what the Lord is communicating. We can grow in our discerning of these communications through time, experience, and God's confirmations.

3. The Audible Voice (see John 12:28-29)

- This seems to be rarer, but God at times speaks audibly to people. In these cases, people clearly hear a voice out loud. Another way this can happen (and perhaps this is more common than an external audible voice), is when there are clear words being spoken, but it is happening internally instead of externally.

4. Dreams and Visions (see Acts 2:16-18)

- Not every dream comes from God, but it is clear in Scripture that God uses dreams as one of the ways that He speaks to us. A dream from the Lord will usually be very clear, memorable, and have a distinct spiritual tone. A vision is seeing something with our spiritual eyes. It can happen as a mental picture, an open vision outside of ourselves, or in some cases in a trance-like state (see Acts 10:9-16).

5. Angels (see Hebrews 1:14)

- We see throughout the Bible that God uses angels for various purposes. One of the ways that angels minister is to bring messages from God to His people.

6. Other People (see 1 Peter 4:11)

- God will often speak through other people. This can come through preaching, the gifts of the Spirit (such as prophecy), simple conversation, or various other ways.

7. Creation/Nature (see Romans 1:20)

- God's glory is revealed in His creation, and He can use it to speak to us. The more we lean into our relationship with God, the more we will recognize His voice through His creation.

8. Any Other Way He Wants! (see Numbers 22:28)

- Though the above list shows the most commonly seen ways in Scripture, there is no exhaustive list of how God may speak to us. God spoke to Balaam through a donkey! He may use unusual coincidences, repetitive words or numbers that we see, circumstances, and other means. Be open to His voice.

Dig Deeper

Read and meditate on Jeremiah 31:31-34. Ask the Holy Spirit to teach you about what it means to know God at a deeper level. Write down anything that God shows you through these verses.

_____
_____
_____
_____
_____
_____
_____
_____
_____
_____
_____
_____

Ask the Holy Spirit to make you more sensitive to His presence and to His voice. Be diligent to seek Him and desire to know Him more. We can't force God to reveal Himself or speak, but we can position ourselves to receive. What are some next steps you can take in knowing God in a more personal way? What are some of the common ways that God speaks to you? If you are not sure, ask the Lord to make His voice clearer to you.

Lesson 6: Knowing God in a Personal Way

_____
_____
_____
_____
_____
_____
_____
_____

For Further Growth

Audio Sermon: Knowing God by Experience

Lesson 7

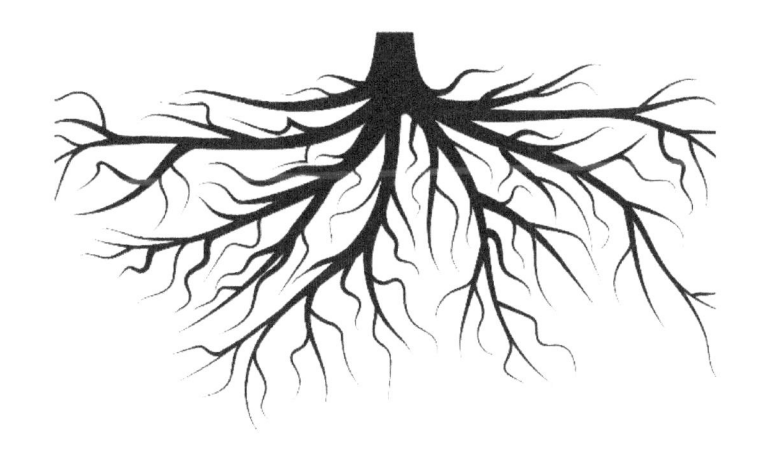

Empowered by the Holy Spirit

Opening Scripture

Nevertheless I tell you the truth. It is to your advantage that I go away; for if I do not go away, the Helper will not come to you; but if I depart, I will send Him to you. (John 16:7)

In the context of the opening Scripture, Jesus is preparing His disciples for His departure from earth. Notice that He says that it is actually to their *advantage* that He goes away. How could this be? What could be better than walking with Jesus on the earth? Jesus explains that it is because when He goes, He will send them the Holy Spirit (whom He calls the Helper).

We can see throughout Scripture that the Holy Spirit plays an integral part in the life a believer and in the life of the church. Yet, He is often neglected and/or misunderstood. There are various names for the Holy Spirit in the Bible: Spirit of Truth, Spirit of God, the Spirit, Spirit of Christ, the Helper, Spirit of the Lord, Spirit of Holiness, and more.

Before we cover more about being empowered by the Holy Spirit, let's look at two fundamental truths.

1. The Holy Spirit is a Person (see John 16:7-8, 13-14; Ephesians 4:30).

- He is not just an impersonal force or a universal energy.

- He is referred to as "He" not as "it."

2. The Holy Spirit is God (see 2 Corinthians 3:17; Acts 5:1-4).

- The Holy Spirit is the third person of the Trinity. There is one God who has revealed Himself in three persons: the Father, the Son, and the Holy Spirit.

- The Holy Spirit has all of the attributes of divinity.

Pause and Reflect

There are various beliefs and perspectives about the Holy Spirit. Some church traditions barely talk about Him or have a limited view of His work today. Others embrace and welcome the work of the Holy Spirit in a more open way.

What is your current understanding of the work of the Holy Spirit today? How have you experienced the work of the Holy Spirit in your life? What does it mean that the Holy Spirit is a *person*?

_____
_____
_____
_____
_____

The Baptism of the Holy Spirit

At the moment of salvation, the Holy Spirit comes to dwell within us. While all believers are indwelt by the Holy Spirit, there is a difference between being *indwelt* by the Spirit and being *empowered* by the Spirit. When John the Baptist was baptizing people in the Jordan River, he pointed to Jesus as the One who would "baptize with the Holy Spirit and fire" (see Luke 3:16). Jesus referred to this as the "promise of the Father" (see Luke 24:49). This baptism of the Holy Spirit is for all believers, and it comes to empower us to live the Christian life and minister to others.

In the early church, we can see that they had experiences of being filled with the Holy Spirit beyond their initial indwelling.

- The indwelling of the Holy Spirit (see John 20:22)
    - The disciples have an initial experience of receiving the Holy Spirit.

- The baptism of the Holy Spirit (see Acts 1:5, 8; Acts 2:1-4)
    - The disciples are filled with the Holy Spirit in order to be empowered.

- Ongoing encounters with the Holy Spirit (see Acts 4:31)
    - The disciples are filled with the Holy Spirit again, giving them boldness to continue to proclaim God's Word.

It seems to be the normal pattern that when believers are initially baptized in the Holy Spirit, they will speak in tongues as the Spirit enables them (see Acts 2:1-4; Acts 10:44-46; Acts 19:1-6). We should expect this to happen today as well.

Aside from speaking in tongues, the effects of the baptism of the Holy Spirit will vary from person to person. Some of the common results are:

- Greater awareness of the presence of God

- More boldness to be a witness for Christ

- Major growth in prayer

- Fresh insight into the Word of God

- Release of one or more of the supernatural gifts of the Spirit

- An overflow of the love and power of God towards others

- Empowerment to fulfill a specific call from the Lord

Pause and Reflect

Have you received the baptism of the Holy Spirit since becoming a believer? If so, how did it impact your life and walk with God? If not, is this something that you are actively pursuing? What has been your experience with speaking in tongues or other supernatural gifts of the Spirit?

Receiving Empowerments of the Holy Spirit

We should seek to continue to be filled with the Holy Spirit: **"And do not be drunk with wine, in which is dissipation; but be filled with the Spirit" (Ephesians 5:18).** If you have never been baptized in the Holy

Spirit, make this a desire and a matter of prayer until you receive. If you have already been baptized in the Holy Spirit, continue to hunger and ask for fresh fillings of the Spirit. There is more!

Receiving the empowerment of the Holy Spirit seems to happen in two primary ways:

1. Waiting on the Lord in prayer

- Jesus told the disciples to wait for the power of the Holy Spirit to come upon them (see Luke 24:49).

- The disciples waited in expectation and prayer (see Acts 1:14).

- The Holy Spirit came in power on the day of Pentecost (see Acts 2:1-4).

- We can follow this pattern by asking God to fill us with the Holy Spirit and then waiting in expectation and faith.

2. The laying on of hands

- There are multiple examples of people being filled with the Holy Spirit through the laying on of hands (see Acts 8:14-17; Acts 19:1-6).

- Gifts of the Holy Spirit can be imparted through the laying on of hands (see 2 Timothy 1:6).

- We can follow this pattern by having trusted believers/ministers lay hands on us and ask for a fresh empowerment of the Holy Spirit.

While there is no formula, there are some key factors to receiving a fresh filling of the Holy Spirit.

- Hunger/thirst (see John 7:37-39)
    - We must be aware of our need and deeply desire to be empowered by the Holy Spirit.

- Faith (see Galatians 3:2)
    - We must recognize that being filled with the Holy Spirit is a gift that comes to us because of the finished work of Christ. We must believe that we will receive.

- Persistence (see Luke 11:5-13)
    - If we do not receive right away, we must persist in asking, seeking, and knocking until we receive.

Dig Deeper

Read and meditate on Acts 2:1-21. Ask the Holy Spirit to teach you about what it means to walk in His power. Write down anything that God shows you through these verses.

_____
_____
_____
_____
_____
_____
_____
_____
_____
_____
_____
_____
_____
_____
_____
_____
_____
_____
_____
_____
_____
_____
_____
_____
_____

Ask God to release a fresh filling of the Holy Spirit in your life. Take time to pray and wait on Him with a posture of expectation and faith. Write down anything that happens or that you sense the Lord showing you.

_____
_____
_____

For Further Growth

Audio Sermon: Receive the Holy Spirit!

Video Sermon: Pentecost and the Fire of God

Lesson 8

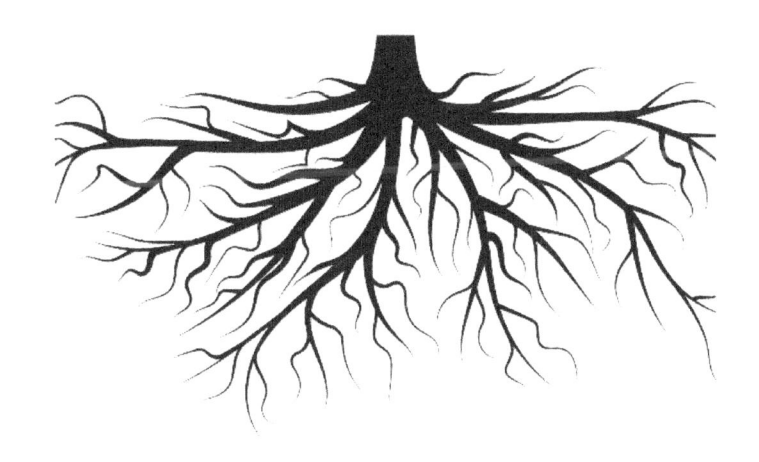

Cultivating the Fruit of the Spirit

Opening Scripture

But the fruit of the Spirit is love, joy, peace, longsuffering, kindness, goodness, faithfulness, gentleness, self-control. Against such there is no law. (Galatians 5:22-23)

The opening Scripture lists what is called the *fruit of the Spirit*. This shows that one of the roles of the Holy Spirit is to produce His fruit in us. The gifts of the Spirit, found in 1 Corinthians 12, emphasize power to minister to others in a supernatural way. The fruit of the Spirit is about godly character in our lives. Fruit and gifts are not in opposition to each other—they go hand-in-hand, and we are meant to walk in both character and gifting. (It is interesting to note that there are nine fruit of the Spirit listed and nine gifts of the Spirit listed.)

- Before we continue, take time to read the greater context of this passage: Galatians 5:16-26

Notice that in these verses, the fruit of the Spirit is contrasted with the desires and works of the flesh. We are born into this world with a fleshly nature that is easily drawn into various types of sin. But when we are born again, the Holy Spirit comes to dwell inside of us and begins to produce His nature in us. The desires of the Spirit and the desires of the flesh are at odds with each other.

This passage teaches two simultaneous truths regarding the flesh that seem to be a paradox:

- For the believer in Christ, the flesh has been crucified.

- At the same time, there is still an ongoing battle against the flesh.

This is similar to our conflict with the devil. While Satan is ultimately defeated through the death and resurrection of Jesus, there is still a battle that rages until the final judgment. Whether in our fight against the kingdom of darkness or our own fleshly nature, it is important to remember that we fight from a position of victory in Christ.

Pause and Reflect

As believers in Jesus, we are no longer meant to be dominated or controlled by the desires and works of the flesh. While we may stumble, the pattern of our lives should be victory over sin and the flesh. Remember, it is by grace that we walk in freedom from sin, not by our own power or effort.

Do you find yourself in a pattern of victory over the flesh? If not, can you think of anything that is hindering you from walking in freedom from sin's power? How would you like to see the fruit of the Spirit more active in your life?

_____
_____
_____
_____

Things that Feed the Flesh

Fruit takes time to produce. You don't plant an apple seed one day and expect apples the next. The same is true with the fruit of the Spirit—it takes time for the character of Christ to be formed in us. Not only does it take time, but it also takes the right conditions and ingredients. One of the keys for bearing good fruit is that we must sow to the Spirit and not to the flesh.

"Do not be deceived, God is not mocked; for whatever a man sows, that he will also reap. For he who sows to his flesh will of the flesh reap corruption, but he who sows to the Spirit will of the Spirit reap everlasting life." (Galatians 6:7-8)

We have a continual choice to either sow to the flesh or sow to the Spirit. If we sow to the flesh, we will reap the works of the flesh, and corruption and death will be the result. If we sow to the Spirit, His fruit will be produced in our lives.

Here are some examples of things that feed the flesh:

- Consuming ungodly and worldly entertainment
- Embracing a self-centered mindset
- Dwelling on lustful, immoral thoughts
- Allowing offense and unforgiveness to fester
- Letting jealousy consume you
- Speaking ungodly words
- Taking on an arrogant and prideful attitude

We have been born again and are no longer to be subject to the ways of our flesh. By the cross of Jesus and the power of the Holy Spirit, we can put to death the desires and deeds of the flesh. **"For if you live according to the flesh you will die; but if by the Spirit you put to death the deeds of the body, you will live" (Romans 8:13).** Being intentional to starve the flesh and feed our spirit is an important aspect of walking in the Spirit and seeing the character of Christ formed in us.

Pause and Reflect

Are there any ways that you have found yourself sowing into the flesh? Is there anything that the Holy Spirit is convicting you about that needs to change? What does it look like to starve the flesh?

_____
_____
_____

Sowing to the Spirit

Instead of feeding our flesh, we must sow to the Spirit. As we consistently sow to the Spirit over time, the fruit of the Spirit will be cultivated in our lives in increasing measure. Here are some ways that we can be intentional to sow to the Spirit.

- Spending time in the secret place of prayer

- Feeding regularly on God's Word

- Obeying the Lord's commands

- Walking in a lifestyle of repentance and staying in the light

- Walking with others in the body of Christ and connecting to the local church

- Learning to recognize and follow the voice of God

- Keeping our relationships pure and being quick to forgive others

- Committing to speak truth and words that are life-giving

Growing in the fruit of the Spirit will happen as a byproduct of walking with God and following His ways. The character of Christ will grow and be formed in us. Others will benefit from the fruit that is being produced in our lives—they will experience the goodness, love, and kindness of God. They will benefit from our patience and self-control. They will be brought into greater joy and peace.

While we certainly benefit from cultivating the fruit of the Spirit, it is ultimately for the glory of God and benefit of others that we develop good fruit. Just as a fruit tree produces fruit for the sake of others to enjoy, we cultivate the fruit of the Spirit so that others can taste and see that the Lord is good! (see Psalm 34:8).

Dig Deeper

Read and meditate on John 15:1-17. Ask the Holy Spirit to teach you and to give you insight into abiding in Christ and bearing fruit. Write down anything that God shows you through these verses.

_____
_____
_____
_____
_____
_____
_____
_____

Lesson 8: Cultivating the Fruit of the Spirit

Ask God to show you how you can be more intentional to sow to the Spirit. Seek for Him to lead you in the next steps to cultivating the fruit of the Spirit in your life. Write down anything He shows you.

For Further Growth

Audio Sermon: Growing the Fruit of the Spirit

Lesson 9

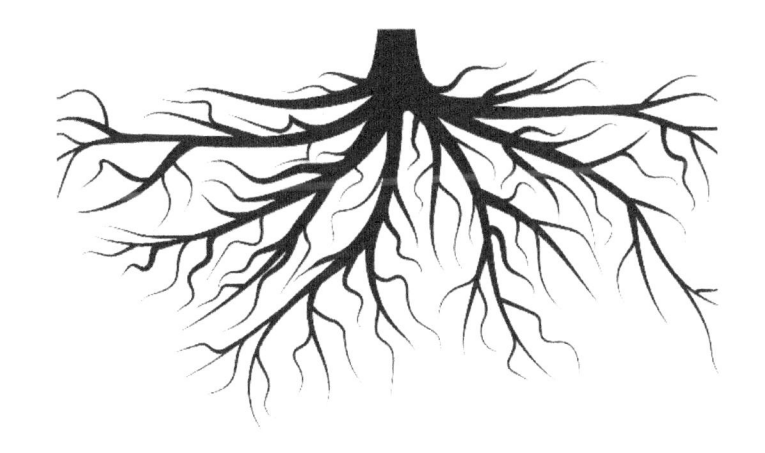

Planted in the House of God

Opening Scripture

Those who are planted in the house of the Lord shall flourish in the courts of our God. They shall still bear fruit in old age; they shall be fresh and flourishing. (Psalm 92:13-14)

Though our relationship with God is personal, it is not meant to be private. There is an individual relationship that we have with the Lord, and this personal connection is absolutely critical. But there is also a community aspect of our relationship with God. We are meant to be connected with other believers in a life-giving way. We are meant to walk in fellowship with other Christians and to take our proper place in the body of Christ.

As the psalm in our opening Scripture states, in order to flourish we must be planted in the house of the Lord. The house of God since the New Testament times is the "church of the living God" (see 1 Timothy 3:15). All believers are automatically connected to the global body of Christ (sometimes referred to as the Universal Church). But the New Testament also describes believers joined together in local congregations.

What makes something a church? Church is not an event and neither is it a building. Church is also not simply any time believers are together—the word *church* in the original language has a more official connotation than that. Churches can be many shapes and sizes and can meet in various types of buildings or homes, but these two variables should be in place:

1. Regular meetings: gatherings for prayer, worship, teaching, equipping, fellowship, etc.

2. God-appointed leadership: leaders such as elders, pastors, and other ministers who have been called and appointed by God to serve in this capacity

Pause and Reflect

Our relationship with God is deeply personal, but it is also meant to have a community aspect to it.

What are some ways that you have benefited from the community aspect of your faith? What has been your experience with the church? Have you had any negative experiences in the past that are hindering you from connecting to a local church in a vital way today?

_____
_____
_____
_____
_____
_____
_____
_____
_____
_____

Descriptions of the Church

The New Testament has various descriptions of the church. Below are several of them, each showing different facets of the nature and purpose of the church.

1. The Family of God (see Ephesians 2:19)

- This speaks to the type of relationships intended for the church. Being born again places us in a new family—the family of God! This does not mean that we must disconnect from our natural family (although sometimes natural family can be the biggest place of conflict when a person becomes a Christian—see Matthew 10:34-36). Believers are meant to be bonded together in love, finding unity in our common Savior and in our common Father in heaven.

2. The Body of Christ (see 1 Corinthians 12:12-27)

- This description signifies both the unity and diversity among the church. We are many members that have various functions and roles, but we are all connected in one body. There are a variety of giftings and callings, and each one of them is important. As the body of Christ, we are to represent Jesus on the earth.

3. The House of God (see Ephesians 2:19-22)

- God is omnipresent, but He also seeks to dwell among His people in tangible ways. In the Old Testament, there was the tabernacle and then the temple. Now, we are the house of God. Individual believers are His temple but so is the church as a whole. When we gather together, we should do so with an expectation for God to be among us in a perceptible way.

4. The Army of God (see Ephesians 6:10-13)

- Whether we realize it or not, we are in a spiritual conflict. The church is a family, but it is also an army. We are given spiritual armor and spiritual weapons to aid us in the battle we are engaged in. Our role is one of advancing the Kingdom of God on earth and pushing back the kingdom of darkness.

5. The Bride of Christ (see Ephesians 5:25-27, 32)

- Being the bride of Christ speaks of both consecration and intimacy. We are to be set apart to God, holy unto Him. We are not to be given to the ways of this world, sin, or false gods. We are cherished by God and are meant to know Him in an intimate and personal way.

Pause and Reflect

Which of the above five descriptions of the church stands out to you the most and why? In what ways have you have experienced the church in these various descriptions? How would you like to see the church more fully exhibit these characteristics?

_____
_____
_____
_____
_____

Why Connect to the Local Church

Out of neglect, misunderstanding, hurt, or disillusionment, some believers find themselves disconnected from the local church. While there might be a season to pull away if there has been abuse or hurt in the context of a church, this should not be the long-term state of a believer.

> **And let us consider one another in order to stir up love and good works, not forsaking the assembling of ourselves together, as is the manner of some, but exhorting one another, and so much the more as you see the Day approaching. (Hebrews 10:24-25)**

Seek God on which local church you are called to be connected to. No church is perfect, but find a church that values the Scriptures and welcomes the Holy Spirit, has healthy leadership, and which you are in support of the vision and direction.

Here are some reasons why connecting to the local church is important.

- Relationship with God is personal but it is also corporate.
    - We are meant to walk together in a community of believers.

- We need each other for accountability, encouragement, and growth.
    - Being isolated makes us more vulnerable to deception and sin.

- God appoints leadership to equip and guide the people of God.
    - We need input and oversight from godly leaders and ministry gifts.

- We discover our gifts and specific function in the Body of Christ.
    - Serving and using our gifts happens in the context of the local church.

Dig Deeper

Read and meditate on Acts 2:40-47. Ask the Holy Spirit to teach you and give you insight into various aspects of church life. Write down anything that God shows you through these verses.

_____
_____
_____
_____
_____
_____
_____
_____
_____
_____
_____
_____
_____
_____
_____

Lesson 9: Planted in the House of God

Are you currently planted in a local congregation? What factors do you use to determine which church to call home? How can you be more connected? Ask the Holy Spirit to speak to you about your involvement in the church and see if He shows you anything. Make sure you are planted in the local church that He has for you at this time.

For Further Growth

Audio Sermon: Connected to the Local Church

Lesson 10

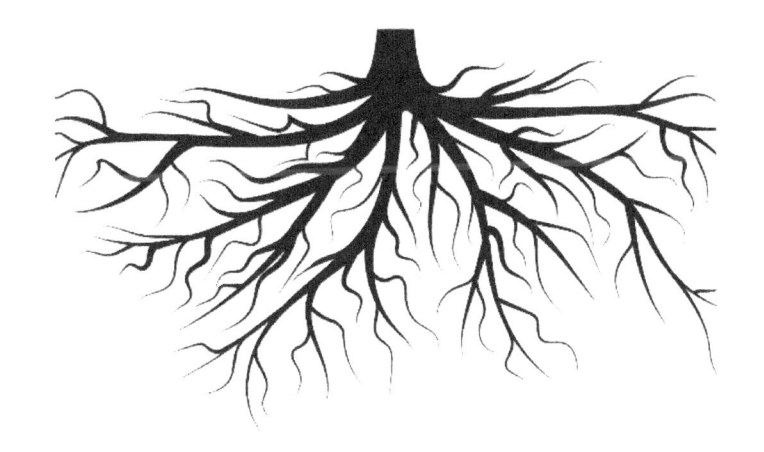

Spiritual Growth through Kingdom Relationships

Opening Scripture

Jesus said to him, "'You shall love the Lord your God with all your heart, with all your soul, and with all your mind.' This is the first and great commandment. And the second is like it: 'You shall love your neighbor as yourself.'" (Matthew 22:37-39)

Notice that the two greatest commandments quoted by Jesus in the opening Scripture have to do with our relationship with God and our relationship with others. There is nothing more important than these.

God is a relational being. Since we are created in His image, we are relational beings as well. Relationships are a part of the building blocks for healthy life and spiritual growth. God uses relationships to help move us further into our destiny and to help us grow in Christ.

Our relationship with others impacts our relationship with God.

- Who we choose to have close association with can either further our growth or lead us down a wrong path.
    - **"The righteous should choose his friends carefully, for the way of the wicked leads them astray." (Proverbs 12:26)**
        - See also Proverbs 13:20

- If we have unforgiveness in our heart toward others, it is a great hindrance to our relationship with God.
    - See the parable of the unmerciful servant found in Matthew 18:21-35

- Dealing with offenses and keeping short accounts with others is key to maintaining our relationship with God and continuing to grow in the Lord.
    - See Matthew 18:15-17; Matthew 5:23-24

Pause and Reflect

Our relationships with others can have a big impact on our relationship with God and our spiritual growth. We should always love people, but there is wisdom in being careful with who we allow to be a close association.

How has your spiritual growth been impacted by relationships in a positive or negative way? Are there any relationships in your life that you need to reevaluate? Is there anyone that you need to forgive or seek to reconcile with?

_____
_____
_____
_____
_____
_____

Three Types of Kingdom Relationships

Our destiny is intertwined with the relationships that God has placed in our lives. The apostle Paul is an example of the power of relationships in our walk with the Lord. His destiny was inseparably linked with Barnabas, who helped connect him to the church after his conversion and who served alongside of him in apostolic ministry (see Acts 9:26-28; Acts 11:22-26; Acts 13:1-3).

Paul also poured into the younger generation (see Acts 16:1-3; 2 Timothy 1:1-7; Titus 1:4). He connected with young leaders and invested in their lives to help them fulfill the calling of God on their lives.

Using the terminology of family, below are three types of relationships that can impact our spiritual growth and calling. While all believers are brothers and sisters in Christ, what I am referring to here are deeper relationships that are ordained by God. They cannot be forced to happen. While they often develop organically, they must be maintained intentionally.

1. Fathers/mothers: those who are further along on the journey and invest in our lives

- These are mentors in our lives. We can learn and grow from our relationship with them, receiving encouragement, instruction, prayer, correction, etc.
    - Consider the example of how Moses raised up Joshua or Elijah mentored Elisha.

2. Brothers/sisters: those who are in a similar place and walk alongside of us

- These are the ones we can walk with, have deep fellowship with, care for, and sharpen one another.
    - Consider the twelve disciples and how they walked together and grew deep relationships.

3. Sons/daughters: those in whom we are intentionally pouring into and investing in

- These are ones that God calls us to disciple and mentor. As we take responsibility to pour into others, we grow in this process as well.
    - As already mentioned, consider how younger leaders such as Timothy and Titus were sons in the Lord to the apostle Paul.

Pause and Reflect

When you consider the three categories of relationships mentioned in this section, can you think of people in your life who fit these descriptions? Who would you consider to be a mentor in your life? Are there specific people that God is calling you to invest in in order to help them grow in the Lord?

_____
_____
_____
_____
_____
_____
_____
_____
_____
_____

Healthy vs. Unhealthy Relationships

Life-giving and godly relationships are part of how we are meant to grow in our walk with God. At the same time, it is important to understand that relationships can also be detrimental to our spiritual growth. Destructive and unhealthy relationships can cause much pain and hinder us from moving forward in our relationship with the Lord and our destiny in Him.

It is vital to identify distinctions between healthy and unhealthy relationships. Just because a person attends church or claims to be a Christian, does not mean that they have the capacity for healthy and godly relationships. We must be careful who we connect ourselves to so that we are not caught in destructive relationships.

Look for these characteristics in healthy relationships:

- An attitude of love, respect, and honor for personhood

- Respect for boundaries and decisions, giving freedom of choice, not forcing of one's own will

- Mutual commitment and investment in the relationship

- Trust built over time through honesty, character, and integrity

Here are some characteristics of unhealthy/destructive relationships:

- Seeking to control others through manipulation, guilt/shame, intimidation, punishment, or other means

- Any type of abuse—physical, verbal, sexual, emotional, spiritual, etc.

- Codependent tendencies and a pattern of being overly needy

- Any type of deception—lying, twisting truth, flattery, etc.

- Any type of sexual contact outside of marriage

Dig Deeper

Read and meditate on Romans 12:9-21. Ask the Holy Spirit to teach you and give you revelation into relational dynamics in God's Kingdom. Write down anything that God shows you through these verses.

_____
_____
_____
_____
_____
_____
_____
_____
_____
_____
_____
_____
_____
_____

Lesson 10: Spiritual Growth through Kingdom Relationships

Ask the Holy Spirit to speak into the relationships in your life, both past and present. Have you experienced unhealthy or destructive patterns in any of your relationships? What are you doing to heal and set boundaries in these situations? Make a commitment to walk in healthy relationships with others and ask the Lord to lead you in this.

For Further Growth

Audio Sermon: How Relationships Impact our Destiny

Audio Sermon: Dealing with Toxic Relationships

Conclusion

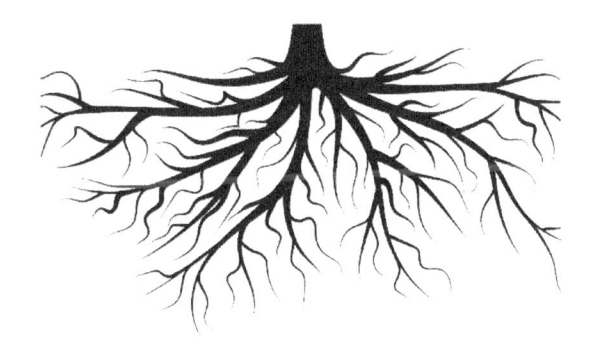

Congratulations on working your way through this discipleship manual! I hope that your relationship with God has been enriched and that you are seeing steady spiritual growth. Continue to give yourself grace while you press forward to grow. If incorporating a new spiritual discipline or growing in a specific area ever seems intimidating, simply ask yourself questions like this: *What is the next step for me to take in this area of growth? What one thing can I focus on to grow in my relationship with the Lord?*

Your relationship with God will grow one small step at a time. As you are consistent in applying the lessons in this manual day by day, your walk with God will develop and flourish. Keep seeking after the Lord—there is nothing more significant in life than loving God and knowing Him more!

Closing Prayer

Heavenly Father, I come to You in the name of Jesus. I thank You for the person reading this manual. I ask that you would draw them into a deeper relationship with You and that You would make Your voice and Your presence more known to them. May they be rooted in Your love, filled with the Holy Spirit, and drawn to You with a greater hunger. Give them a fresh grace to enter into the secret place to pray, seek You, and be with You. Give them a deeper love for the Scriptures and more revelation of Your Word. Help them to apply what they have learned so they may continue to grow in Christ and know You more. In Jesus' name, amen!

Bonus Resources

Check out the following resources to help you grow in the Lord and be equipped for service in the Kingdom of God.

Online School: School of the Secret Place

A List of E-courses and Online Schools

Book: Restoring the Ministry of Jesus

Book: How to Minister Deliverance [Training Manual]

A List of All Jake's Books

Jake Kail Ministries YouTube Channel

About the Author

Jake Kail was called to ministry in college after a life-changing encounter with God. He is passionate for the presence of God and to see His kingdom come and will be done "on earth as it is in heaven."

Jake is the author of multiple books, including *Setting Captives Free* and *Restoring the Ministry of Jesus*. He speaks at churches, conferences, retreats, and other events, preaching and teaching with a demonstration of the Holy Spirit's power.

Jake lives in Lancaster, PA with his wife Anna and their kids, and serves as the apostolic leader of Threshold Church.

Visit Jake's ministry website and blog:

www.jakekail.com

Like and follow Jake's page on Facebook:

www.facebook.com/JakeKailMinistries

Follow Jake on Instagram:

@jake_kail

Made in the USA
Las Vegas, NV
11 March 2025